DIVORCE
The Middle-Aged Man's Survival Guide

By
Zackary Richards

ARI PUBLiSHING

Ari Publishing

P.O. Box 602

Lake George, NY 12845

Library of Congress copyright #636972771

DIVORCE- The Middle-Aged Man's Survival Guide should be viewed as a self help book for middle–aged men who suddenly find themselves in an adversarial relationship with their spouses. This is not to suggest that these stories are from the marriages of the people associated with this book or from my own. They are instead a compiling of events that I discovered occur so often and with such commonality in the breakup of long term marriages that they should, for the benefit of both parties, be brought to light.

Chapter 1

First, let's lay out some ground rules. This book is not for those of you who stupidly screwed up your marriage. If you were cheating and she dumped you, well, you knew the risks going in. Same goes for you who became alcoholics, gamblaholics, drug addicts, couch potatoes, wife beaters and deadbeats.

Likewise for those who treated your family like serfs or indentured servants. Again, you brought it upon yourselves.

This book is not to infer that all wives are malicious, vindictive, conniving psycho's who believe all their troubles, failures and disappointments would never had occurred had they not gotten married.

There are plenty of normal, decent women out there.

This book isn't about them.

This book is intended for the men who worked steadily over the last twenty-plus years, helped their wives raise the kids, attended all their plays and sporting events. Mowed the lawn, took out the garbage, fixed the sink, was patient and understanding during that 'time of the month' and fully expected to be married for the rest of their life.

Then out of nowhere and for no discernable reason, the women they loved, honored and cherished for the last two-plus decades can't stand the sight of them and will do anything, (yes, and I mean anything) to get out of the marriage.

If this is what you're going through, then you need to read this book. Why? Because I have been where you are now and you're going to need to know what to expect, how to react, how to defend yourself and how to cope with what might very well be the most difficult period of your life.

Chapter 2

When Wives Attack!

How it begins…

It usually starts somewhere in your late forties through your fifties. By this point you and your wife have survived your children's teenage years and they are leaving the nest. You've barely managed to keep your sanity as your wife battled menopause and the hormonal rollercoaster that went with it. You've endured all that life can throw at you and you're still standing. You're approaching the final few laps of your working life and if all goes well, you and the missus should be able to retire and enjoy the fruits of decades of hard work.

Congratulations!

In many cases that is the end of the scenario. Husband and wife ride off into the sunset and live happily ever after.

For the rest of us there is one last hurdle. One last battle and hopefully, one last victory.

But if you intend to get to the victory part, you'd better be prepared. Because everything you believed about your marriage, everything you thought you knew about your wife and your relationship… is about to be proven wrong.

And for years, yeah *years* afterward, you are going to wonder, "Just what the hell happened?"

Can my marriage be saved?

You might not have any say in that. Remember it takes two to make a marriage and if she wants out, then that's it, regardless how you feel. On the other hand, it may be possible that she is having health issues or hormonal problems and so, if she suddenly starts acting hostile and irrationally, convince her to see a medical professional. You don't want to discover after the divorce that she was suffering from small strokes or a brain tumor or some other physical ailment. Then, once the health issues are addressed you can move forward with a clear conscious, because—and this is something else you need to understand right away—if she has become difficult, vindictive and just a miserable human being to be around, it's very likely she's doing it on purpose.

Women don't like to be seen as 'bad guy' in any relationship, so if she's looking to rid of you she'll be increasingly difficult with each passing day until <u>you</u> finally cry Uncle and say: "I want a divorce!" This way she can tell everyone, it was your idea and she is just an innocent victim.

How can I tell if my wife is looking to end the marriage?

Unless we're talking infidelity, it's rarely just one thing. When a woman wants out of a marriage she makes preparations, takes small steps to test the waters. Sees how it feels to not have you in her life. See if she likes it.

So she begins distancing herself from you. One of the most common examples of this is her occasionally sleeping in one of the now empty bedrooms. When you ask about it, she claims it's because you snore, or her back hurts, or she doesn't want to wake you when she goes to the bathroom. There's always some excuse.

You go along for a time but complain when her sleeping in the other bedroom has evolved into an every night thing.

She capitulates, usually because you have agreed to wear some device that will stop your snoring, or have bought a new (and usually expensive and bigger) bed, nevertheless, as the weeks pass, she spends more of her free time in that empty bedroom, begins moving her things into it, starts referring to it as 'her bedroom', as in, "What are you doing in my bedroom? Or "I must have left it in my bedroom."

Naturally you want to put an end to this and get things back to normal. Having endured the menopause thing, you figure that it's her hormones kicking in again so you make an extra effort to be thoughtful. You buy her things and take her places in the hope that if you just ride it out, life will go back to the way it was before.

But it doesn't.

Oh sure, she'll give in some nights just to keep the peace but then begins slipping off to bed early and when you go to join her, you'll find she's in 'her' bedroom and is sound asleep. (It really doesn't matter when you find her there, be it 2 minutes or 2 hours after she goes to bed, she will always be 'sound asleep') And of course if you wake her and ask why she's sleeping there instead of your joint bedroom, she'll act like you're making a big deal out of nothing and then ask with a real attitude, "Why couldn't this conversation waited until morning? Or, "Why was it so necessary for you to wake me up from a sound sleep?"

You're an insensitive jerk, you know that?

At least that's what she wants you to think, because insensitive jerks don't get sex. Insensitive jerks get the cold shoulder so they can reflect on what they've done.

What you don't realize is she wants these arguments, wants to be at odds, because for as long as she can be angry at you, she doesn't have to have sex with you.

So she'll intentionally start trouble. For example, she'll start locking 'her bedroom' door at night. She'll say things she knows annoy you, and when you call her on it, she'll pretend you misunderstood and why are you always jumping down her throat?

She will also **do** things, for example, vacuuming in front of the television at a critical moment during a sporting event. And when you ask her to stop, well, you've just bought yourself another argument, buster.

"It seems no matter what I do, you're always yelling at me!" she says all teary-eyed as she yanks out the plug and storms off.

Of course you have to follow her and apologize (which makes you miss the highlight play of the game.)

You go through your 'I'm sorrys, I didn't mean to raise my voice. I do appreciate all that you do around here.' "It's just that you stepped in front of the TV just as they started the big play."

"I think you care more about your stupid (fill in sport here) than you do me!"

You see, now she's upset again and it's all your fault. Looks like you won't be getting sex anytime soon, Mr. Insensitive Jerk.

Don't kid yourself, she knew exactly what she was doing and got the result she wanted.

As guys, we have an innate need to fix things. While the wife is playing you like a fiddle, you are under the impression you have done something to hurt her feelings. Figuring that's the case, you immediately try and fix it.

What you don't realize is while you're running around like a puppy eager to please, behind your back she's taking a baseball bat to the relationship, not only hoping to kill it, but make its demise look like your fault.

My wife could never be that devious.

Wanna bet?

What you need to understand is the sweet woman, the loyal companion, the trusted friend and lover is gone, most likely forever.

If you've raised a daughter you might better understand what I'm talking about. Remember when she was a little girl? When her eyes would light up at the sight of you? How she would run into your arms and hug you with all her might? Remember how she thought you were the greatest thing in the world? The bestest, bestest, Daddy?

Remember her going through puberty? Remember what she was like as a teenager?

Remember her dismissing you as a blithering imbecile, rolling her eyes when you spoke, battling you at every turn?

You never expected your sweet little girl to change like that did you? And fortunately, over time things worked out and the two of you resumed your relationship. My point here is when some women go through "The Change", they don't change back.

Chapter 3

Stop blaming yourself

Most men, when the wife suddenly turns on them, begin soul searching, trying to figure out what they did to make her hate them so.

This process can go on for months. And most guys make every effort to correct whatever they suspect is causing the rift in their marriage. They run to the gym to get back in shape, cut back on watching sports, become more romantic, take her to new and exciting places etc.

Sometimes that works.

Most times it doesn't.

And on many occasions, the reason for her hostility has nothing to do with you.

Nothing to do with you <u>at all</u>.

She's angry because *she* has done something so despicable and disloyal behind your back that every time she sees your stupid face, she's reminded of what she did. So now she feels guilty nearly all the time and it's all because of you!

Many women grow up believing that someday her knight in shining armor, her Prince Charming, will appear and whisk her away to some magical land where she will have everything she ever wanted and live "Happily Ever After".

A fantasy, true, but they are also intensely pragmatic and take well thought out steps to make it happen. Unlike men who can become brainless zombies under the spell of a beautiful woman, most women decide by their teens what type of man they want. After their hormonal 'bad boy' infatuation, they set their sights on the guy who is stable, strong, independent and most importantly, headed for success. A man who can provide for her and the children she will give birth to, one who can protect her and who will work himself into an early grave for her.

This is what women want.

And as you've probably learned over the years is whatever a woman wants is something she fully expects you to provide.

So now, twenty or so years into your marriage, what *does* she want?

That's simple. She wants you dead.

That's right. SHE WANTS YOU DEAD!

This way she can pretend to mourn your passing, be the grieving widow who is center-stage at the funeral as well as the strong matriarch, who, with her grown children by her side, will stoically soldier on now that you've shuffled off to the Great Beyond.

Then, after she collects on the insurance and what she considers the appropriate amount of time has passed, she will sell the house and begin the 'Happily Ever After' phase of her life.

Oh the joy of having the freedom and the money to do whatever she wants, whenever she wants!

Unfortunately, there is a drawback. Something keeping her from having that 'Happily Ever After' she so justly deserves. And what is that snag?

Why, it's you, you selfish bastard! How dare you keep all her dreams from coming true! She did her part. She had and raised YOUR children, kept YOUR house, put up with YOUR disgusting and perverted sexual desires. Why she's a living saint and now that the kids are grown and she no longer needs you, you have the gall to continue living!

I told you they were pragmatic.

So what do you do?

Unfortunately, some of you, facing a future of loneliness, alimony, illness etc, will foolishly grant their psycho wives' wish.

DON'T.

Trust me, life gets better. Just hold tight, you can get through this. It will be horrifically brutal but you will survive. I know because I've done it. So have others. You can too.

Chapter 4

Cover your Ass.

As men, we have a societal disadvantage. Remember that old sexist saying; Little girls are made of sugar and spice and everything nice, like rainbows and sunny days, and ice cream, whereas boys are made out of Snips and snails and puppy dog tails, old socks, used condoms and roadkill.

The point being is that whatever your wife accuses you of, it will be believed.

Why? Because society teaches us that **ALL MEN ARE BRUTES**! *And all women are loving and caring and beyond reproach.*

Why is this? Well, one reason is that a woman will readily portray herself as meek, defenseless and non-confrontational. They will tell anyone who will listen the details (whether real or imagined) of the abuse she has endured.

Men don't. If their wife screws around, runs up debt, drinks, or physically abuses them they won't say a word. Their world is hard enough, and the last thing they need is for people to think of them as a pussy-whipped weakling.

Outdated stereotypes.

Here in the 21st century we are quickly doing away with archaic stereotypes and generalities about people's heritage and religions. As the world grew smaller it became obvious that not all Irish drink, not all blacks can dance, and not all Asians excel at math.

The problem is that the sugar and spice versus the snips and snails myth still persists.

Much too often are women given the benefit of the doubt simply because we are psychologically indoctrinated from birth to believe that all women are good and nurturing. To a little boy, his mother is often the most important person in the world. She takes care of him, encourages him, and unquestionably loves him. The image of women that most men take into adulthood is that they, at least from their experience, can do no wrong.

Men are perceived differently. From the first day in the schoolyard we learn that any show of emotion is an invitation to be bullied. You learn to defend what is yours because if you don't, it will be taken it from you. You never, cry, whine or complain. Whatever the hardship, whatever the misery, you are taught to remain stoic and never show you're hurting. If you are the oldest, then you are responsible for the protection of your siblings, and in some cases, your mother when the old man becomes furious at her for reasons never revealed.

Perception is not reality, and accepting stereotypes is dangerous.

There is no court of law in this country that would allow any prosecuting attorney to claim that the reason the construction job wasn't completed on time was because the contractor was Mexican and as we all know, all Mexican's are lazy.

Nor would they allow any prosecutor to claim that the reason expensive equipment disappeared from a jobsite was because one of the workers was Italian and as we all know, all Italians are members of the Mafia.

Yet a wife can accuse her husband of any outrageous crime and on her say-so alone, he can be arrested and placed in jail.

My friends, we must put an end to this stereo typical belief because it allows women to commit the most treacherous deeds without any fear of reprisal.

In the movie "As Good as It Gets," a woman asks Jack Nicolson, playing the part of a writer, how he is able to create female characters so true to life. He replies. "I think of a man, then take away reason and accountability."

Damn accurate.

Here's an example: One day at work, I came upon a group of females listening to one of their co-workers talk about her impending divorce. Normally, I would have walked past but stopped and kept out of sight when I heard her say, "I've been trying for months to get that sonavabitch to hit me but he just won't do it. He's such a pussy. Why just the other night he took me out for dinner, said he wanted to try and patch things up. So I figured here was my chance. So I started an argument and just as things got heated, I said loud enough for everyone to hear, 'Look, I just can't take it anymore you limp-dick faggot.' Well, his face turned beet red and he was so mad I was sure he was going to jump over the table and belt me but no, he wimped out again. If I can just get him to hit me hard enough to raise a bruise and get the cops involved, I can walk away with just about everything he owns."

Yeah, that happens more often than you think.

Here's another.

After twenty-five years of marriage a man comes home and finds a note from his wife that reads. I don't love you anymore. I have left and am not coming back. Don't try to find me.

The man is devastated. He thought things were fine. Their kids were in college, the house was paid off and over the years he had put a substantial amount in their joint bank account for their retirement.

Yeah, I said joint account.

And because they had opened the account under "John OR Jane Doe instead of John AND Jane Doe, she was able to withdraw all the money from the account without his knowledge or consent and then go off and travel the world.

Okay, just one more.

Again we have a middle-aged guy who has no idea why his wife of 22 years suddenly can't stand the sight of him. We'll call him Bob. One day Bob notices that his neighbors, people he has known for decades are avoiding him. And his daughter—

whose college tuition he is paying—won't return his calls. This continues until one night, he receives a call from somebody obviously drunk. Before Bob can even say "Hello" the drunk tells Bob how lucky he is to be married to such a wonderful woman, then berates him for giving her gonorrhea. Before Bob can tell the caller he has no idea what he is talking about, the caller hangs up.

Turns out Bob's wife had been giving not so subtle hints to her female neighbors that he had given her a venereal disease. Having already decided to divorce him, and wanting to keep the house, she figured if she could get the neighbors to turn against Bob, he wouldn't fight to keep it.

Okay, okay, this is the last one, I promise!

After 25 years of marriage 'Sally' decides to have her younger, attractive and sexually permissive sister over for a couple of days. Her visit just happens to begin on the husband's poker night.

About ten minutes after Sally's husband staggers in, having consumed a night's worth of beer, Sally announces that it's been a long day and that she's going to bed. Husband offers to join her but Sally suggests that he and her sister spend some time catching up.

About ten minutes into the catching up part, the topic has somehow switched to sex and she's describing in considerable detail, just what turns her on.

Husband's heart begins to race and he can't wait till it's his turn to tell her what turns him on.

Fortunately, all the excitement has burned off the alcohol and his "Warning, Will Robinson, Warning!" systems are coming back on line. He suddenly asks himself, why would his sister-in-law, who is very close to his wife, be trying to seduce him, when her beloved sister could appear at any moment and catch them in the act?

It's amazing how fast a man can sober up in these situations.

So, he waits for her to stop talking and then says, "Hey, check this out." And as the sister-in-law wonders what he's going to show her, he quietly sprints into the next room and surprises his wife, who is waiting on the staircase, fully dressed, with camera in hand.

There are few things as damning in a divorce as having your soon to be ex-wife, submitting photos to the court of you and her sister going at it.

Okay, moving right along. Here's a mistake that might get you killed.

As you approach middle age and come to terms with your mortality, as a man, you feel the obligation to provide for your family's financial future should you no longer be around. So, after convincing your wife of the necessity of you increasing your life insurance death benefits, you contact your agent and take care of it, then relax knowing your family will be financially secure. You see it as a responsibility, proof that you are a good husband and parent. She sees it as the means of someday having the "Happily Ever After" she's always dreamed of.

Remember women expect to get everything they want and get very angry when they don't. If you've ever seen the television show 'Snapped,' you will know exactly what I'm talking about. Each episode features a middle aged woman charged with killing her husband. And in each episode, regardless of how damning the evidence, she will turn on waterworks and act as if somehow, *she* is the victim.

To remind you of how badly the cards are stacked against men, remember the show is called, 'Snapped' which in itself suggests that the women who committed these acts couldn't possibly be cold-hearted killers, no! Somebody must have done something terrible to that poor innocent woman that drove her over the edge. (Guess who?)

What I'm saying here is you need to be careful. If she cooks your meals and you suddenly come down with flu like symptoms (poison)… Or if you keep a gun in the house (it accidently went off in her hand)… Or if she calls you and goads you into an argument over the phone (it's being recorded, just ask Mel Gibson)

So if your long term marriage has gotten to the point where it resembles some of the examples you've just read, find out exactly how much you're insured for and check and see if there are any life insurance policies in your name that you're not aware of.

You should also get any and all gun(s) out of the house. This is important. Statistics confirm that a homicide is 5 times more likely in a domestic dispute if there is a firearm in the house. So if your home has become a hostile environment and tempers are flaring regularly, all it takes is for one of you, in a blinding fit of rage, to do something that will cost you or her your freedom, your family, and quite possibly your life.

It doesn't have to be a permanent thing. You can always bring them back or replace them at a later date when, one way or another, the conflict is resolved, and your life has returned to normal.

But for now, make sure they are in a place where you can't get at them. Trust me, this is one piece of advice no one has ever regretted following.

I once heard a comedian say: "If you never seriously considered killing someone, then you've never gone through a divorce."

That's truer than you'd like to believe.

Chapter 5

What brought this on?

So let's look at the situation, overall you've been a good husband, father, provider, upstanding member of the community, and all around good guy, so why does she suddenly hate you?

There are a million theories, woman in the work force with their own money and line of credit, menopause, aging etc. The one I subscribe to is the theory that we, as men, used to die earlier, usually in our mid–fifties. Now, that's all changed. There are strict laws to prevent accidents in the workplace, advanced heart surgery, chemotherapy, car seatbelts, Strict DWI laws, all of which are extending the average man's lifespan.

Some women feel that once the children they wanted are raised and have left the nest, you should too. Just leave behind your weekly pay check, pension, the house, the car and the savings account.

You see, because women can never allow themselves to be viewed as the bad guy, or the cause for the marriage breaking up, they become delusional. They convince themselves that they are victims, deserving of compensation, of a reward for 'putting up with you' for as long as they did. And for all the things she did for you, and the sacrifices she made, and all the sexual acts she performed to please you.

What is never mentioned are all the things you did for her. How you went to work every day, sometimes two jobs to take care of her and the children. How you put up with her monthly mood swings, shopping binges, and all the 'chores' she came up with to fill your weekends. Or all the times you moved the living room furniture around because she decided that it, "Just didn't look right." Or how, had you never married and had kids, you would have saved enough money by now to retire ten years early. Or how the constant stress of living with a menopausal woman and raising kids going through adolescence over the last few years has destroyed your digestive system.

Oh the terrible things she accuses you of.

He doesn't listen and /or talk to me anymore.
Of course she blames you but often she brings this on herself. Now that the kids are gone, she has to adjust to a new situation and like any new situation; it's difficult, a little frightening and takes time getting used to. So, she begins prattling about anything that comes into her head and it never occurs to her that you might not be interested in what her Aunt Clara is going to quilt this summer. And why should you be? Has she ever shown any interest in your fantasy football team, or what the over and under is on the Super Bowl? Of course

not, you know this and you're considerate enough not to waste her time by bringing it up.

That doesn't apply to her. She believes you should hang on her every word and show real interest because apparently everything that pops into her dopey head is of vital national interest and should be listened to with rapt attention.

Then there is the other case, where no matter what the topic, she's always contradicting, disagreeing or using your comment as a way to start an argument. So you learn to keep your mouth shut.

She however, views your silence, not as a means of keeping the peace, but as a mean-spirited way of freezing her out by giving her the silent treatment.

Well, two can play at that game, Mister.

She's losing her hearing.

She begins turning up the radio or television because according to her, no one speaks clearly anymore. Especially you and she's positive you're doing it on purpose just to annoy her. Why else would you mumble all the time and then, when she politely asks you to repeat what you said in a clear voice, you continue mumbling, and when she asks again, you shout at her for no reason whatsoever.

You see, it never occurs to her that asking you to repeat yourself over and over is annoying. She doesn't grasp the concept that it's <u>her</u> disability and that you shouldn't have to stop everything you're doing or watching to retell what she didn't hear. What she should be doing is thanking you for helping her cope with her disability, not act like it's your fault she has it. And heaven forbid you suggest she get a hearing aid. ("Those things are for old ladies, are you saying I'm an old lady?")

And when she finally does admit that she has a problem, it's still your fault for not looking directly at her when you speak (which makes for considerable excitement when driving) and for not enunciating properly so she can read your lips.

It's also your fault when what she <u>hears,</u> isn't what you <u>said.</u> You'll be in the doghouse quick enough when she asks "how come you're late?" and you reply, "I had to stop for gas." But what she hears is "Stop being a pain in the ass."

You miserable bastard, how could you talk to her like that!

You don't appreciate all she's done for you.
Husbands are accused of this all the time. Wives' constantly complain that they do so much for their husbands: "Look how nice I decorated the house for you, how I keep it clean and all the meals I cook for you. Look at all the nice clothes I buy for you, how I raise your children for you" and on and on it goes, so much so that even you start to believe it.

But it isn't true.

Let's look at the facts. All the furniture you have was probably picked out by her. Same goes for the drapes, rugs, dishes, etc. Everything is arranged the way she likes it from those little soaps in the bathroom to the welcome mat at the front door. The house reflects her tastes and her tastes alone.

Why?

Because most guys couldn't care less if the drapes are green or blue, or what the silver pattern is, or what style of furniture she decides on just as long as you get to have a recliner and a big screen TV.

And let's face it, she doesn't keep the house nice for you, she keeps it nice for herself and to show off to her neighbors and girlfriends. Most guys don't care if there are a few dishes in the sink, or an empty pizza box on the coffee table, or if they left the cabinet door open, or if the rug needs vacuuming. If they lived alone, all those thing would be taken care of eventually and the place would not, as she claims, turn into a garbage dump without her.

As for the nice clothes she buys for you, well again it's for her benefit. You are her 'Ken" doll and will be dressed as she sees fit to impress her friends and neighbors.

Because most guys dress for comfort, they will wear the same collection of shirts, pants, underwear, and shoes until the day they suddenly and mysteriously disappear.

But you liked those clothes!

Yeah, like that matters.

And as for cooking your meals and raising your children, well let's be blunt. She cooks because she needs to eat, as do the children and since if she's cooking anyway adding an extra serving for you is no great sacrifice on her part, and should she cook just for herself and the rest of the family and exclude you, that just her subtle way of letting you know you're not welcome anymore. And lastly, that nonsense about her raising your children, she needs to be reminded that they're her children too.

It's a woman's prerogative to change her mind.
This concept is completely absurd yet women often use that catch phrase to renege on agreements and responsibilities. For example, you ask her to go out with you on a specific day and time and she agrees. You purchase tickets to a show, make reservations at a fine restaurant then book a moonlit cruise to follow. Everything is going just fine but then just minutes before you're scheduled to pick her up, she calls and says she can't make it. An old friend from college showed up and she's promised to show her the town.

But what about the arrangement with you?

Well it is a woman's prerogative to change her mind!

What do you think would happen if good buddy#1 scored two tickets to a championship game, a meet and greet with the players before the game and drinks in the VIP lounge afterward and asked you to come as his guest. You agree, then at the last minute, you bow out because good buddy #2 invited you to a skiing weekend and you like skiing better.

How many trips to the dentist do you think you would need in the days that follow?

Bye-bye sex

Here's a common trick women use to get out of the marriage. They pretend to be angry with you for something they won't divulge and refuse to have sex with you.

"Well, if you don't know what you (said/did) I'm not going to tell you!"

How many times have you heard that one?

What is really happening is she has decided to cut you off sexually because she no longer requires it and doesn't care that you still do. (Or maybe she is getting it elsewhere).

Here again she is testing the waters. Seeing how long she can go without being intimate. She is already envisioning her life without you. And to her it is oh, so much better!

So now you're going without sex for weeks, and sometimes even months and when she finally agrees, it's begrudgingly and you can tell she's looking for any excuse to get out of it.

During this time you say nothing to your buddies. Nothing to anybody. It's too embarrassing. You're alone in bed and unloved. And while you're trying to cope with this fresh hell you've been saddled with, she's getting ready to make her move, perhaps even hoping that you will cheat on her.

Here's something you should know and it's important. When your wife no longer loves you, she no longer cares who you sleep with, especially since she has no intention of ever having sex with you again. So when you complain about the way she's treating you; and that as a man you need sex, she might suggest that you get yourself a 'mistress'. This way you can have all the sex you want and leave her alone.

WOW! Being able to have a mistress with your wife's permission??!! How lucky can a guy get?! It's too good to be true!

Be very, very careful. True, there are some women who wouldn't mind continuing to live as your wife but without the sex, but in most cases, this is merely permission for you to go out, buy your weapon of choice then proceed to beat yourself to death with it.

Why? Because once word gets out that you're seeing someone on the side, (almost always it's a younger woman because younger women still need and enjoy sex) the wife can put on the 'dutiful and loving wife betrayed by carousing husband' dog and pony show.

And so, once again you're the bad guy. No mention is ever made that the 'dutiful and loving wife' has been withholding sex from the husband, or has been recoiling from his mere touch, and hasn't so much as kissed him in over a year.

Nah, why bring that up? No one will believe it, she will deny it and you will look like a pitiful slob who can't get sex from his own wife.

Seriously, who is going to believe you when you testify during the divorce proceedings that your wife gave you permission to take a mistress, especially when she is sobbing hysterically and vehemently denying it?

Chapter 6

Red Alert

If you believe that your marriage is in serious trouble, or if she's acting peculiar and you suspect she's making plans to divorce you, see a divorce lawyer.

Almost all first consultations are free and by seeing one you will learn the most important fact of life that you will ever need to know.

WHAT YOU BELIEVE IS MORALLY RIGHT AND WHAT IS LEGAL HAVE ABSOLUTELY NOTHING TO DO WITH EACH OTHER.

NOTHING!!!

I'll give you an example. In New York State (laws in other states may vary) if your wife clutters up say, the guest room with her nick-nacs, old clothes, shoes, magazines, exercise equipment, etc. and you pack it up and move it to the garage because it's becoming a fire hazard, you will hear from your wife's attorney who will inform you that removing your wife's possessions from the home is considered abuse. All items are to be returned immediately and if you remove any other of her belongings, an Order of Protection will be filed against you and you will be ordered to vacate the premises immediately or be sent to jail.

Yep, that can happen!

Let me preface my next statement with this disclaimer. **I AM NOT A LAWYER, NOR AM I QUALIFIED TO OFFER LEGAL ADVICE.**

That being said, if you sense something is wrong, if things between you and your wife have been going from bad to worse for a considerable period of time, or if you suspect that your wife is looking to get out of the marriage…

GO GET THAT FREE CONSULTATION IMMEDIATELY!

Here's why.

As I said earlier, because women can't stand to be thought of as the bad guy, they become delusional. Over time they convince themselves that you are heartless, insensitive, cruel, vindictive and abusive and she's only filing for divorce because you have made her life so miserable she has no other choice.

You've done nothing of the sort but she's convinced herself that it's true. She has to believe it or she'll have to face the reality that she's the troublemaker, that she's the home wrecker and that's it's her own selfishness that is putting her family through this heart wrenching process.

There is a saying regarding divorce and it goes like this:

Women marry men thinking they will change, but they don't. Men marry women thinking they won't change, but they do.

The danger for you is in the second sentence. Nearly every man I talked to about going through a divorce after 20 plus years of marriage said they were blind-sided by the rage and hatred directed toward them by their ex-wives, astounded by the false accusations, and floored by the outrageous demands for compensation.

Nearly all said, "I still can't figure out what I did to make her so damn angry."

They said the woman they divorced was somebody they had never met. The woman they married was kind, loving, gentle, and considerate. She was his helpmate, lover and trusted companion. The woman he divorced was a lying, grasping, vindictive harpy who, if he had just met her, he would run off after the first two minutes.

The reason most men get reamed by their wives' lawyers is because they don't realize that their wives' HAVE CHANGED. The person you loved so dearly and trusted so much now feels you're responsible for every misfortune that has ever befallen her. She has convinced herself that her life would have been perfect had she never married you and for that she wants to rip out your heart and ram it down your throat.

The one time love of your life is now the enemy. Accept it, nut up and press ahead.

This brings us back to you seeing a lawyer.

Find out how experienced he is, how many years has he been specializing in divorces. How many cases is he presently handling? Will he personally handle your case? (Some big law firms hand off cases to younger, less experienced lawyers after you pay the retainer.) If you are not satisfied with the answers, go to a different law firm and keep looking until you find the right fit. Remember, your wife's lawyer is paid to tear you apart, and take everything she can get from you. It's her job to put a legal bullet in your head then rifle through the pockets of your corpse. So make damn sure the person you hire to protect you is up to the task.

Because he will be defending you against the most outrageous accusations and outright lies ever told about you!

Here is the second most important thing I will tell you:

Do exactly what your lawyer tells you!

The above line is so important that I'll repeat it.

Do exactly what your lawyer tells you!

Do not deviate from the script, don't ad-lib, don't wing it. Tell him the absolute truth and don't ever say or do anything your attorney tells you not to.

EVER!

If you've hired a lawyer you trust, someone you feel confident will properly defend you, then **LET HIM DO IT.** He knows the tricks your wife's lawyer is preparing to pull. He knows she will make every effort to make you look like an angry and dangerous man. She will bait you; try to lure you into a legal trap. Allude that you physically and sexually abused your wife behind closed doors. Indicate that you may have cheated on her with several women. Suggest you may have had improper contact with the children. Anything that will push you over the edge, anything that will make you ignore your lawyers advice and storm over to your wife's residence to confront her. To demand that she tell the truth…

…and give your wife's lawyer the necessary ammunition she needs to have an Order of Protection filed against you.

But! But! But! But!

No buts, follow your lawyer's instructions regardless of how unfair it seems. He's done this many times and knows what to expect. You don't.

And yes, I know that if you only had a chance to talk to your wife privately, the two of you could sort things out.

Do you really think so? Or are you just looking for the opportunity to tell her exactly what you think of her? Because if you go in there angry, I guarantee it will backfire and you will regret it.

One the other hand, if you have come to terms with her wanting a separation from you and simply want to get it over with, if she's agreeable, give it a try, but do it in a place where there are people around, like a restaurant. Keep in mind the possibility that she is recording your conversation. And if she tries to goad you into an argument, it means she never had any intention of trying to find common ground, so just smile and say, "I'm sorry we couldn't agree to terms," and leave.

Something for both of you to consider, the longer this drags on the more money the lawyers get. So it's in their interest to play this out for as long as they can.

Yeah, buddy, you're getting blasted from both sides.

And sometimes, it's better to cut your losses and start over. The goal of this book is to alert you to the possible dangers and to help you avoid being caught unprepared and taken advantage of. So if she offers a deal you can live with, take it, sign the papers and move on.

Are you being served?

One of the most despicable tricks your wife's lawyer might use will be to have you served with the divorce papers while you are with your friends and/or relatives.

Say for example, it's Thursday night and you're at the bowling alley with your team and playing for the local championship. Midway through the third frame a guy wearing a bowling shirt walks up to you and asks if you are Mr. So-and-so.

You reply that you are and he hands you an envelope, says "You've just been served," takes your picture with his cell phone and walks away.

In shock you tear open the envelope and remove the papers.

The papers say your wife is suing you for divorce, and the reasons thereof.

Baiting tactics like the above are fashioned to make you act irrationally. You storm over to where she's staying and bang on the door and demand to see her till the cops arrive and drag you away. Or you get drunk and make a threatening phone call. Throw a brick through her window.

And why the hell shouldn't you? You have every right to be furious. Imagine her humiliating you like that! And in front of your friends no less. That miserable bitch!

Okay, well you need to calm down and place a call to your lawyer. Explain what happened and do what he tells you.

I'll say it again. **DO WHAT HE TELLS YOU!**

His advice may contradict everything you are certain must be done immediately and without hesitation but if you do what he tells you, it will keep you out of jail and may make it possible for you to keep your house.

Don't let her play the crazy card.

Because of her bizarre behavior over the last few months you begin confiding to your buddies that's she's crazy, simply out of her flipping mind. One minute she's all 'let's let bygones be bygones,' the next she's cursing you out. One night she sleeps in the guest room, locks the door and puts a chair up against the knob. The next morning, after her shower, she slips into your bedroom while you're sitting on the bed, and without a word, drops the towel and starts gathering her things in the nude.

At this point you don't know whether to shit or go blind.

Do you make a move on her? Is she trying to seduce you, or looking to collect semen so she can claim you forcibly raped her?

Then there are those moments when she acts like a teenager going through adolescence. "I'm going to do what I wanna do, when I wanna do it!" she bellows at the top of her lungs, then thunders off and slams the door of 'her bedroom'.

She uses each and every opportunity to strike out at you, doesn't need a reason, just does it.

Just what the hell are you supposed to do?

Here's what you do. You keep your mouth shut. Don't tell your buddies, don't tell her family, don't tell anyone because in many states you cannot divorce a woman who a judge deems is in need of psychiatric care. In addition, you may be held responsible for the cost incurred. Most times the crazy act is used to get you to say you want a divorce, but you running your mouth about it may result in your paying for her medical care for the rest of your life.

Make a list

Buy a notebook, and every time you remember some horrific event she put you through, <u>you write it down</u>. That's right, write down each and every one of them with as much detail and accuracy as possible! Why, because in the hustle and bustle of everyday life these things get forgotten. And it's very important that you remember what brought you to this place and who is responsible, because somewhere down the line you're going to need ammunition when she pulls the innocent victim routine and accuses you of every despicable act under the sun.

This information will also be especially helpful on those nights when you're alone and wishing you had someone to be with, and start considering calling the ex.

True, you may be so angry now that you think writing down what she did is unnecessary because it has been seared on your heart with a branding iron.

Do it anyway. Because you won't always feel this way and there will be times when you'll need to be reminded what you went through. This is not hateful or vindictive action to take. The notebook is there to prevent a poor memory from allowing what you suffered through before to happen to you again.

A while ago I saw a bumper sticker that read:
Tis better to have loved and lost…
Then to remain married to that psycho!
Words to live by.

Chapter 7

The Separation

When it becomes apparent your marriage is in trouble, people will begin choosing sides. Most will side against you because society has trained us to believe that all men are sex-crazed Neanderthals and all women are innocent Polly Purehearts. Your kids will distance themselves from you, as will your neighbors. If some of your friends were originally her friends, they will likely side with her. If one of your friends is married to a woman who is friends with your wife, say goodbye to him too. If you happen to be good friends with her brother, remember blood is thicker than water and as Vito Corleone once said, "You never take sides against the family."

This also goes for the mother and father-in-law, should they still be alive. Regardless of how close or how much they thought of you in the past, because of their daughter's accusations, you are now as welcome as a turd in a punch bowl.

So let's start with how she'll sabotage your relationship with your friends and neighbors. At the next party or get together she will begin your character assassination by staging the 'he's an asshole but I won't tell anyone why' routine, to draw people to her side. This is where she acts like she's doing all she can to not appear horrifically pissed–off, but she's so angry, it's just plain impossible.

Wow! You've must have done something really terrible!

Throughout the evening she's stomping around with her arms folded and a scowl on her face while you're trying to figure out what the hell got into her. When people eventually ask her what's wrong, she'll turn to you with a look of disgust, and say, "Why don't you ask that asshole?"

At this point you're wondering, "Why am I suddenly the bad guy?"

Well I'm going to tell you. What she is doing is creating an event she's hopes will stick in people's heads. Long after the food is eaten and the party is over, she's betting they'll remember that you did something terrible that day (they won't remember what, but that doesn't matter) and are the obvious cause for the trouble in the marriage.

Now as for your kids, even though they are adults, or at least close to being adults, they are going to want to know why you and their mother are suddenly fighting all the time. Because, let's face it, if you are separating and talk of divorce is being bandied about, it's going to affect them and their relationship with you.

Determined to get the children on her side, she'll step into the role of the 'suffering martyr'. Oh the suffering and pain she has silently endured for their sake. And the absolutely despicable things you have done to her—BUT BEING A GOOD WIFE--

she refuses to reveal what they are, for she is forever loyal and true, regardless of the fact that you're such a heartless prick.

Very much like a scene from one of those over acted 1920 silent films.

Action!

The children gather around their mother, who is sitting on the floor sobbing with head in hands. A sad piano plays in the background.

"Oh, mother dearest, what has happened? Why do you weep so?" the children ask.

Mother places back of hand on forehead, looks upward. "Do not worry, children. I'll be all right. The only thing that matters to me is that you're happy and healthy. I'm sure your father does too, well… (Meaningful pause) At least in his own way."

"Father? Was it father who made you cry?"

Mother wraps her arms around the children. "That's not important. I'm sure he didn't mean to. Sometimes your father, well… (Another meaningful pause) I shouldn't talk about it. You're much too young. This is a matter between me and him. Just know that I will always love you and do everything in my power to protect and keep the family together."

The children hug mother tightly. "We love you so much, mother and we always shall."

Then the littlest one, with the big eyes and the cutest smile says, "I hate father so much for making you sad!"

Mother caresses the child lovingly and says, "Now, now, remember, he is your father so you mustn't say bad things about him."

Then the boy says, "Very well, mother, we shall do as you ask but only because we love you."

Cut and print.

Women are notorious for this tactic. She pretends to have been savaged by something you did but is far too loyal and forgiving to actually say what it was. If pressed she will allude to it being something sexual but too personal to discuss.

This is usually done in the weeks and months just before she files for divorce. While you're still dopily running around hoping to work things out, she's lining you up in the crosshairs.

Collateral Damage

There can be other victims of the breakup other than you and the kids. Here's an example:

When the children were in middle school they began pestering the parents for a dog. The father was not enthusiastic knowing he'd be the one out walking it at night and in the cold but the wife sided with the kids so they picked up a young German Sheppard and brought him home.

He was a good dog and not much trouble, so it looked like everything was going to turn out all right.

But then…

As the kids moved into their teen years, they wanted less and less to do with the dog. So over time the dog became very attached to the wife, and in effect, became her dog. (Not surprisingly, the husband still got stuck walking the pooch at night and in the cold)

Then the husband got a promotion and the position required that he live closer to the job. The husband wanted them to move into an apartment or to rent a house, unfortunately, none of the places available allowed dogs. When the suggestion was made of giving the dog away, the wife flatly refused and said that if they couldn't rent a place that allowed dogs, then they would have to buy a house.

Having friends who owned houses and knowing the amount of maintenance necessary for the upkeep, the husband was strongly against the idea. He wasn't at all handy and didn't want to spend his weekends doing maintenance and repairs. However, with any mention of giving up the dog causing a flood of tears from the wife and pleas from the children, the husband capitulated and they found a house, took out a mortgage and moved in.

Fast forward 18 months.

With one kid in college and the other busy with high school and her social life, the wife has become the dog's entire world. It is at this point when she announces she wants out of the marriage and has rented an apartment in another town.

The apartment doesn't allow pets but she doesn't tell the husband. So he figures once she moves all of her stuff out and they sign the separation agreement, she'll pick up her dog and that will be that.

Well, all of her things do get moved out, everything except the dog.

So the husband calls the wife, but she never answers. So he leaves messages asking when she's going to pick up the dog.

She doesn't call back.

He contacts her attorney and explains the situation.

A day or so later, the wife shows up furious. "I'm here to pick up the dog!" she says.

The dog is ecstatic to see her. He had been pining for weeks and had run away several times to search for her.

"You're very selfish, you know!" the wife says to the husband as she puts the leash on the dog.

"What are you talking about?"

"You know damn well I don't have room for a dog in my new place and besides, they don't allow dogs there."

"First of all," the husband replies, "I've no idea where you live and you said when you left you would take the dog with you. That was the deal! So why did you rent an apartment you knew didn't take dogs?"

"Because I needed to get away from you!" she snaps, "and now I have to spend money I haven't got, to have the damn dog put down!"

"What do you mean, 'have the dog put down?' He's only eight and has a lot of good years left in him. What you need to do is find him a proper home."

"Well I don't have the time, I'm very busy."

The husband watches as the dog jumps all over with the joy off seeing her again.

"C'mon," she says, yanking the dog's leash. "Let's get this over with."

Then, with the look in her eye telling him that she would gladly have had him 'put down' too if she could get away with it, the husband takes the leash from her. "Get out!" he tells her.

"If I leave without that dog," she threatens, "he's your dog."

He pulls the dog away from her, he points to the door. "I said go!"

She turns and storms out.

In the months that follow the dog spends most of his time at the window, anticipating her return. When he finally realizes she's never coming back, he develops health problems, loses weight, and becomes lethargic. The husband tends to all the dog's needs but they never really bond. It's clear the dog resents the husband and the husband resents the dog,

All because of the wife.

Within two years the dog is dead from a broken heart

Give credit where credit is due

After decades of marriage, the average married couple has credit cards in their own name and maybe one or two jointly. It doesn't matter because the monthly payments for all the cards are withdrawn from their joint account.

In this case the married couple decides to stop renting, buy a house that needs repair, and do the work themselves. She purchases all new furniture and appliances with her credit card and he installs new siding and builds a deck, paying for the materials with his.

While the husband is busy fixing the place up, he receives a letter from his credit card company offering him a brand new optimum platinum card with very low interest rate on transferred balances for 36 months. With both their present credit cards carrying interest rates in the mid teens, the wife says that this is a perfect opportunity to save a lot of money and suggests they transfer all the balances from their other cards to the new one.

To him, that does sound like a good idea, so he does as his wife suggests.

Fast forward six months.

All the repairs have been completed, the house looks terrific and out of nowhere the wife announces that she wants out of the marriage, has rented an apartment, has taken 'her half of their money' out of the savings account and wants him to sell the house that he has spent the last six months fixing up and give her half of the profits.

The house is appraised at nearly double what he paid for it but it won't sell. Without her income he can barely make the mortgage payments and because she transferred all her outstanding balances to his credit cards, he can't even make the minimum payments, His interest rate skyrockets and his credit score crashes and burns.

He later discovers it was his wife who had seen the credit card offer while logged on to the internet under his name and clicked on the 'send me more information' button.

So in the end, husband has lost his wife, all his money, his excellent credit rating, any possible profit on the sale of the house and is buried in debt.

The wife however, has a healthy bank account, an excellent credit rating, has moved all the new furniture and appliances into her new place, has no outstanding debt and a great new life to look forward to.

Just something you might want to keep in mind.

Chapter 8

Just like starting over.

I'm not going to get into the complexities of who left and who stayed. For the sake of continuance, let's say that because she was so anxious to put an end to the marriage, she's the one who moved out.

So now you're legally separated. Check with your lawyer regarding the laws of your state regarding your socializing. Getting involved with other women during the trial separation may cost you plenty should you eventually get a divorce. Also set some ground rules regarding contact with each other. Don't drive past her new place unless it's absolutely necessary, and don't call her at home or at work without invitation. It can be perceived as stalking and frankly you got enough to deal with.

So now you're alone in the house. This is where the reality sets in. Whatever property she was awarded is being, or has been, removed and taken to her place. Make sure this happens in a timely fashion. You don't want her showing up unexpectedly and using the need to pick up her stuff as an excuse to check up on you or to find out who you've been seeing.

Have your lawyer put into the separation agreement that she has say, thirty days to remove all her belongings from your place of residence, after that time she loses all claim to them.

Once done, leave her alone and get on with your life. She was the one who brought this about and you making up reasons to call, or sending her a birthday card isn't going to change anything. The whole idea was for her to get rid of you; she's done that and is moving on.

You need to as well.

In some instances as the months go by she'll discover she doesn't like the single life. Discovers all those things you did for her was a lot more important than she realized. She may even call you in tears, asking for a second chance, telling you she made a horrible mistake.

She will say she's sorry, so very, very sorry and embellish it with blubbery sobs and pauses to catch her breath. "Can you ever forgive me?"

Let's take a moment to review.

Over the last year or so, she has, in an emotional sense, run you over with a truck, then stopped, put it in reverse and backed over you, and repeated this over and over until she felt that she finally got even with you for all the terrible things you did to her in her delusions and hallucinations.

Does a heartfelt, "I'm sorry," make up for all that?

The question YOU need to ask yourself is, "After doing everything in her power to get rid of you, why the change of heart?

Be very, very careful here because her attempt to patch things up may have nothing to do with you.

Maybe the rich guy she was hoping would be husband number 2, dumped her and with no new prospects, she's panicking at the possibility of spending the rest of her life alone.

Maybe the temporary settlement isn't covering her excessive spending and she needs to hop back on the gravy train. Or maybe she has come down with a physical ailment that requires surgery and is going to need someone to take care of her while she recovers.

So ask yourself, "After you solve her problems, what's preventing her from firing up the old Ford F-150 and coming at you again?

If the answer is nothing, and you still agree to take her back into your life, then all she will have learned from the experience is that no matter what horror she inflicts on you, what misery or disloyalty she lays at your doorstep, all she has to do is cry and plead and lure you into bed and you'll forgive her anything.

And when a new guy catches her eye, or you pay off her credit cards, or you nurse her back to health, she will hug you and kiss you and tell you you're the most wonderful man in the world…

…then dump you because, again, she's got what she wanted and doesn't need you anymore.

If she is genuinely sorry and serious about getting back together, make it clear that before you even consider letting her back into your life, she must first make amends for what she did to you. For example, if in the separation agreement, she insisted in getting your guitar and amp, even though she doesn't play, those items need to be returned. Any money the court made you pay her that was not rightfully hers, she must pay back. Any money you spent for your lawyers and legal fees for the separation she initiated, she must reimburse you.

In addition, she has to contact all the relatives, friends and your children and tell them the accusations she made about you were lies and were used as a means of getting out of the marriage.

After she has done all these things, then, if you feel so inclined, let her back into your life. The point is, her 'saying' she's sorry amid hysterics and tears doesn't mean a damn thing. It's what she 'does' that counts.

Remember making amends isn't revenge, it's making her take responsibility for her actions and if she isn't willing to do that, then nothing has changed.

Dating

If there are no legal issues with you getting back on the dating circuit, then by all means do so. But proceed cautiously. Because somewhere down this road you are very likely to date

The five women you meet in hell!
(Said with a wink to author Mitch Albom)

You haven't done this in a long while and are seriously out of practice. And just like there are predatory men out there hitting on unsuspecting women, there are predatory women out there too.

The first, you're probably familiar with.

The Goldigger

She's the type who will find you utterly amazing, she'll gaze in awe when you tell her of your accomplishments, she'll laugh at your jokes, tell you you're a fantastic lover and no, you don't need to use a condom because she's on the pill and doesn't want kids anyway.

My friend, to her you are merely a future divorce settlement pay off, for which she's willing to marry you, put in the prerequisite three years and squeeze out a child, (I guess she forgot to take her pill that day, oops!) then divorce, and saddle you with alimony and child support. What's worse, you are perceived by society as a 'dirty old man' because you're over fifty and deserve to be punished for 'forcing her to have your child' at your age.

Why you contemptible old pervert!

Up next:

The Revenger!

Women your age, who are presently unmarried, (unless she is widowed), are usually unmarried for a reason. Take the case of the Revenger, this poor victim spent her youth and decades in an affair with a married man, then for reasons she cannot fathom, he dumps her and takes up with a much younger woman!

The Revenger can't wait to have a guy like you fall in love with her so she can make you pay for what that other guy did! Remember, your emotional well-being is insignificant; all that matters is that she gets it out of her system and feels better.

Then there is:

Jekyll and Hyde

These women are walking time bombs. They are nice, personable and make you feel that you can tell them anything. But before you do, find out how many friends she has. If her only friends are relatives and she has absolutely none at the work place…

Run.

Jekyll and Hyde women build up anger and store it like gunpowder over days, weeks and sometimes even months, then when full, she waits for you to say something she can intentionally misconstrue as an insult, then fires both cannons in the form of verbal abuse.

In that explosion she'll sadistically rip you a new one. Reveal everything you told her in confidence, your every secret, then ridicule your every shortcoming.

Finally, after she has completed her verbal evisceration, she'll break down into tears and run off as if she is the injured party. Meanwhile you're standing there in shock trying to figure out what you did to set that off.

Well you didn't do anything. That's simply what the Jekyll and Hyde personality does. This rage builds and builds until she can't hold it in anymore, then she verbally attacks, hoping her crocodile tears and victim personae afterward is convincing enough to let her get away with it.

Again it's not important that she humiliated you, revealed your confidences and did her best to hurt you. All that matters is that she feels better now.

Now let's visit:

The Damsel in Distress

Here's how this one works. You meet a woman who is witty, friendly and fun to be with. You'd like to date her but she tells you she's in a troubled relationship that she can't get out of because of (fill in problem here, doesn't matter what it is, it doesn't figure into the mix)

What matters is she's yearning to be free but that (monster, ogre, bully, again it doesn't matter) she's living with won't let her go.

Well just before you slip into your Knight in Shining Armor personality and set out to resolve all her problems, here what lies ahead.

After meeting clandestinely for a certain amount of time, you fall in love with her and want to bring your relationship out into the open. No more of this sneaking around.

She wants to, needs to, but can't. She doesn't make enough money to get a place of her own, her job pays little to nothing, her car is on its last legs and she needs him to keep it running, and of course, she doesn't want to be a burden to you because she cares about you too much!

He's where you take her into your arms and insist she move in with you. You'll get her back on her feet, why you're The Knight in Shining Armor!

Fast forward.

You now understand why the person she was living with made absolutely no effort to convince her to stay. In fact, he damn near packed her bags.

Why, because in order for her to solve her problems, some effort is required on her part. You found her a good paying job. All she needed to do was show up every day for the paid six-week training period. Unfortunately, her sister got sick and she took it upon herself to go over there every day to feed her dog, and therefore washed out of the training course.

Well, she couldn't let the dog go hungry till after she got home from training now could she?

You set up a payment system on her computer that will automatically pay her bills when they come due. This way she can avoid all the late charges she is accruing.

Oops! She forgot to deposit the money in her account. She was going to but a friend called and she 'lost track of time'

You keep trying to straighten out her life and she keeps screwing it up.

Guess who she is describing as an (monster, ogre, bully) to a guy she just met?

And last but not least

The Searcher

As mentioned earlier, if a woman has never married, or has never been in a serious long-term relationship, there is probably a good reason. When women talk about men, they often say "All the good ones are taken."

This applies to women too.

In the case of the Searcher, she'll claim that she 'almost' got married a couple of times but the plan fell through for some reason or another, (that part is never made clear.) What's so dangerous about the Searcher is, as you fall in love with her, it'll appear she's in love with you too.

You'll take cruises, go to great restaurants, travel together, and make passionate love. For months things are fantastic. You start seriously thinking about a future with this woman.

Then, out of the blue, she dumps you.

The reason she gives is a hodge-podge of new age blather that doesn't address the question. Nonsense like, "I realize now that I'm not ready for a real relationship, or I need more me time so I can better find out who I am." Then just shrugs and walks off.

The Searcher is an emotional sociopath. She did enjoy the time you spent together, loved the lovemaking and the adventures you shared but now that it's clear you are becoming emotionally attached to her, she needs to cut and run.

Tootle-ooo, lover, it was fun while it lasted. Don't call me, I'll call you.

Chapter 9

Life without her.

Okay, she's out, the papers are signed and the marriage is officially over. The adrenaline from the battlefield has subsided and you're on your own.

This is where it gets rough.

For one thing, two plus decades of your life has been seriously altered. You no longer have a wedding anniversary date. All the family traditions you joyfully celebrated over the years no longer exist. The in jokes, the shared memories, and all the happy times you spent with each other can never be looked back upon without feelings of betrayal and resentment.

You don't have a family anymore. Your team has been disbanded.

Sure your kids will come to see you but only after they have the 'which parent do we see on what holiday' debate and train themselves to remember what not to say about the other parent. (You've got a new girlfriend and Mom's started drinking.)

Your family albums, once the source of countless happy memories are put away. As are the videos of family vacations, graduations, anniversaries.

Mementos of places you went together, special places you two enjoyed. Gone.

You stomach seizes up when the song you chose for your wedding is played on the radio. Your wedding ring has become a symbol of failure. Your wedding album, all those pictures of relatives and friends, all having a great time, meaningless.

If she had died, and your religious faith prescribes to an afterlife you could look forward to seeing her again, to loving her again.

No chance of that now.

All gone.

So what do you do?

First decide what you WANT to do. Many of your friends will attempt to set you up with someone, which is fine if you're up for it. But firmly tell them no if you're not. Don't let them give you that 'you got to get right back on the horse' nonsense because over the last year or so you've been beaten down, betrayed and abandoned and may be in no shape to jump back into the social scene.

You'll know when you're ready.

Beside rebound romances rarely work out. You're the injured member of the herd and the predators are circling.

The ex carved a huge hole in your heart and it hurts like hell and all you want to do is get your life back to the way it was. So you start dating right away and let's say you're fortunate enough to meet someone new who's kind, thoughtful and considerate. She's comforting and understands what you went through; maybe she's been through a divorce as well.

You consider moving in together…maybe consider the possibility of marriage somewhere down the road.

On the rare occasion this works out. BUT, most times it doesn't because;

You're still grieving and are not thinking with a clear head.

You haven't established a new and independent life yet.

Because of the divorce, you're suspicious, jealous and paranoid.

Jumping into a new relationship just because you're lonely will very likely lead to another bitter breakup.

Let's dispense with the he-man crap for the time being. The person you loved, trusted, shared your life and most innermost thoughts with, turned on you and with no remorse whatsoever, destroyed everything the two of you built up over twenty plus years.

This hurts! This really hurts! You did nothing wrong. You obeyed the rules, turned down the sexual come-ons offered to you over the years, held a steady job, kept the bottle at bay, was always there when she needed you and stuck up for her against all comers.

And for what? Why is your life now in the toilet?!

Yeah, I know, but that's the way it is. Not right, not fair and not deserved. But here you are so, what's your next move? I received my answer to that question while watching the movie, the Shawshank Redemption. In it there is a line that goes, 'You have two choices, you can get busy living, or get busy dying.'

Those are <u>your</u> choices.

I decided to get busy living.

And that's what you're going to do!

What to watch out for

If you live in the same area as the ex, sooner or later you will run into her and her new beau. When you see them in some store being all lovey-dovey, it will feel like a punch in the stomach. If you can leave without her seeing you, do it. You don't need the aggravation.

However, what if she sees you, walks over and asks how you're doing?

You nut up and say you're fine.

Then she introduces you to the boyfriend.

And in goes the knife and…yep there's the twist.

At this point you're likely to have an overwhelming urge to punch the boyfriend in the mouth and start wailing on the ex with the nearest blunt instrument.

Not that I'd blame you, but that would be a mistake, so don't do it.

Because your ex is still delusional, she's under the impression that because she got what she wanted and is now happy, you should be too. In fact, you should be happy that she's found someone. Right?

Okay, stay calm. He's what I suggest you do.

Say hello to boyfriend and shake his hand. Unless he's a former best friend or buddy, he probably doesn't have the slightest idea what went on between you and the ex. He's probably only started seeing her and is on that high that comes with a new relationship.

She, on the other hand needs to be reminded of what she did, and what a pathetic excuse for a human being she is. There is no need for violence, yelling or verbal abuse. What is needed is closure.

So you turn to the ex after shaking the boyfriends hand, lose the smile and say something to this effect. "In the future, should we run into each other I would appreciate it if you act like we never met. Because every second I'm in your presence I'm reminded of the cruelty, disloyalty, and hatefulness you exhibited during our divorce. I truly wish I never met you."

Then walk away.

Reality usually has little effect on delusional people so most likely after you leave, she'll just shrug and go back to chatting with her boyfriend but that's all right, you told her exactly what you thought of her and by thunder it needed to be said!

But shouldn't we keep the doors of communication open?

Nope, absolutely not. That was okay during the trail separation but no longer. Yes there will be times that will require you to be in each other's presence, like when one of your kids gets married or the christening of a grandchild, that sort of thing. And on these occasions simply smile, be pleasant, make small talk with her whenever necessary and when the event is over, leave. You don't need to say goodbye to her. Good-byes are for friends, relatives and associates. She is none of those. Remember that.

In addition, keeping the lines of communication open often leads to trouble. Why? Because the more you see of her, the longer it will take for your memories of her to fade. The second problem is the more contact you have with her, the more likely you'll start having feelings for her again (that would be no surprise, you have decades of shared experiences together) and wouldn't it be just great if you two fell in love again and started to believe that the divorce was a mistake? Why it was just middle age crazy, happens all the time! So you get married again, have a second honeymoon, pick up where you left off. Everyone is so happy to see you two back together.

Then six months into the new marriage, she starts sleeping in the guest room, she hasn't been in the mood for sex for over a month, and why have you started to pick on her again...

Wasn't all the misery you endured the first time enough? Do you really want to put yourself in a position where it could happen again?

Not if you're still in your right mind. When you're done and the final papers are signed, cut off all contact. Take her phone number off your contact list, make no attempt to find out where she lives, and if someone offers to tell you, tell them you aren't interested. If you're the one who moved out, don't tell her where you live and ask those in contact with her not to divulge your address. If you get mail addressed to her, have it returned to sender. Take her name off everything that does not belong to her. If a membership is in both your names, have them change it. Contact the person who does your taxes and ask him what changes you need to make now that you're divorced.

Your previous life is over. Treat it as such.

Whatever you do, don't crawl into the bottle!

Although I don't have any facts to back this up, I firmly believe most men who became alcoholics later in life, did so after their marriage and family broke up. And why not, it's very tempting. Each night you come home to an empty house or apartment. You cook yourself some crappy meal or bring in greasy fast food. You have no one to talk to, no one to tell how your day was, and no one to wrap their arms around you and welcome you home. It's just you, feeling depressed, miserable, betrayed and alone.

But wait! There is something right over in that liquor cabinet that will chase the blues away, or even better, there's that little tavern right around the corner where everybody knows your name, well maybe not yet, but by the time the night is over, they will.

Fast forward.

To avoid dealing with the loneliness of your empty apartment you've begun stopping off at that little tavern every night and having your dinner there. After your meal you order some drinks and strike up a conversation with the guy sitting next to you.

After a few months the place has become your second home and although you're not aware of it yet, you've begun your downward spiral.

Because you have work in the morning, you don't allow yourself to get sloppy drunk, just buzzed enough to so when you get home, you fall fast asleep and don't have to think about how miserable your life has become.

But since you're no longer in your physical prime, you don't immediately bounce back from a night of drinking. At this point, it takes until the afternoon before you're yourself again.

But that only applies to the recovery time following one night of drinking, but now since you are stopping in there every night and have a hangover every morning, by mid week it's all you can do to keep your eyes open, let alone do your job properly.

So your productivity falters and your boss notices. Although you always make it to work on time and are dressed professionally, your morning haggard look is raising concerns.

The higher-ups begin to wonder if your most productive years are behind you. Perhaps it's the early signs of impending illness. Maybe the time has come to start looking for your replacement.

During the next round of downsizing, you're let go. You get a good severance package and figure with all the experience you've accumulated over the years, you'll have a new job in no time.

Except that doesn't happen.

You discover the job market isn't as friendly as it was say, fifteen years ago. In today's business world new technology is being introduced every day and is advancing at a furious pace and you know what they say about 'old dogs and new tricks.'

Frustration leads to heavier drinking. You're now out of a job for months with no new prospects in sight. Your drinking has now led to serious bouts of depression. Your life is spinning out of control. You get cited with a DWI. Your family and friends are urging you to go into rehab, but you don't have that kind of money. You've been out of work for over a year.

How did this happen. What did I do to deserve this?

Here's my advice, take it or leave it, your choice.

The bottle is your best friend right up until the very day it kills you.

Facing depression

Because depression is a serious medical condition, you should see a doctor immediately if you are experiencing any of the warning signs and especially if you are having thoughts of suicide, because it may not just be the blues over losing your marriage, you might be seriously ill and in need of medication.

But if it's just the blues and a feeling of being 'down in the dumps', keep in mind that accidental prescription drug overdose is becoming a serious problem. So before you go the prescription med bandwagon, consider trying a healthy diet, exercise and joining a support group. And if that doesn't work then see your physician and follow the anti-depression regimen prescribed, because many anti-depressants do help and just might be exactly what you need to make it over the hump and back to your normal life.

Just remember, having that type of medication in your medicine cabinet is like having a gun in the house. Used properly, it can save your life. Used improperly, it can kill you.

Don't bad mouth the ex.

"Wait a second," you say. "Why the hell not? Especially after what she did to me!"

Okay, calm down, cowboy. I'm not arguing the fact that you got every right to go out and tell everyone in the whole damn world what a lying, miserable, vindictive…

But remember, by openly attacking her, you are making your kids look bad. She gave birth to them and what bad traits you attach to her, is by blood, going to be attached to them.

The second reason is that people aren't stupid. True, they too often believe what they want to believe, but over time it's the consistency of your actions that will outweigh any accusations.

And if your kids are keeping their distance following the breakup of your marriage it's mostly likely because of your ex's portrayals of the monstrous things you've done to her, (Details of which she will never reveal).

Fortunately, over time they begin to notice the irregularities in the ex's accusations. And that some of her thinly-veiled claims of abuse simply aren't realistic, and certainly not something their father would do, or even be capable of.

So when your kids ask to hear your side of the story. Say something like, "Your mother and I had a happy marriage for over two decades. Together we had beautiful children and a happy home. Unfortunately, sometimes even long, happy marriages end and you're given no choice but to accept it. All I've ever asked is when your mother accuses me of acting in a certain way, I'd like you to think back to our lives together, and ask yourself, "Is that something your father would do?" And if the answer is no, then think twice before believing it.

Trust me, they will.

Chapter 10

Starting a new life

So, just how does one do that? How do you start a new life?

First, you be completely honest with yourself. Just what do you need at this point? Do you need to scramble for money because of the divorce? Do you need female companionship? Do you need to get back in shape?

Find out what you want, then find out what you need to do to get it.

"But what if I don't know what I want?" you ask.

Well then, my friend, it's time to saddle up and go on a quest. You've spent the last quarter century or so tending to the needs of the wife and kids, now the time has come to tend to your own.

For many of us finalizing a divorce is like coming out of a year-long coma. You're unsteady, confused, anxious and suspicious. You're leery of trusting anyone and can easily fall into a pattern of self destruction.

"Why should I watch my drinking? It's not like anyone cares!"

"No, screw diet and exercise. I'll eat whatever I want, whenever I want."

"My blood pressure is high because I got screwed by my ex, I don't need any damn pills."

Why bother taking care of yourself? After all that time and hard work you're back to square one. Only difference is that you're older, less attractive, less resilient, and are probably taking a couple of meds each day to ward off the afflictions that come with age.

It took nearly a year following my own divorce but I finally woke up and began following the same advice I'm going to give you here.

First you need to regain your health. Divorce takes a lot out of you both emotionally and physically. First get a physical and make sure you're healthy enough to begin an exercise regimen, then join a gym and go every day. That's right, every day. They usually aren't expensive and are worth the money.

Any activity a person does consistently for over a month becomes a habit. That is true for bad habits as well as good. In addition, exercise keeps you occupied; your mind off your problems, helps you sleep and reinforces your self- esteem.

Next eat healthy foods. You don't have to become a health nut, just stay away from the fatty stuff you've been filling up on because you feel lousy all the time. Lose the potato chips, greasy fast food and other crap smothered in cheese.

Many nutritionists say you should eat a serving of greens, mushrooms, onions, seeds/nuts and berries each day. Yeah, I know it sounds like a lot of hippy-dippy, new age nonsense but there is solid science behind it. Those five food types provide the right combination of vitamins and nutrients your body needs to function properly. Just eat that combo once a day, just like you would an oat based cereal at breakfast to lower your cholesterol, and within a few days you'll notice the urge to stuff your face will lessen. That's because your body is getting the proper fuel to do its job and no longer needs to get you to eat something in the hope that you'll pick the right thing.

It doesn't have to be a life-long commitment, just stay with it until you've gotten yourself into decent shape and have begun your new life.

Okay, she's gone and I'm on my own. What's the next step?

Bury yourself in your work.

Since you don't have to concern yourself with the wife and kids anymore, and you no longer dread going home after work like you did before the separation, now is the perfect time to start honing your skills by taking courses and making it known that you're ready for a promotion. And if your recent unsteadiness due to the divorce has killed any chance for moving up the ladder, then it's time to actively search for a new job. Maybe in a new town or city. Remember you're starting a new life, don't let the old responsibilities and routines hold you back.

Develop hobbies.

Make a concerted effort to try new things and master new skills, then join groups that meet to discuss those hobbies.

I know you're probably hesitant about this. I know I was, but I made a deal with myself to find things I felt I could get interested in, then go to these group meetings at least three times in a row. I figured I would have a pretty good idea of what these people were like by then and could make an unbiased decision on whether I wanted to continue attending.

I discovered I lost interest in some of those hobbies over time and developed an even stronger interest in others. But the most important part is that I kept busy and didn't dwell on the divorce and what I had lost. I started focusing on what I was gaining.

Make <u>NEW</u> friends.

I'm not suggesting you abandon your old buddies but this is a new life you're building and you need to stock it with new people. The problem with old friends is they are such a core part of your old life, conversations regarding your shared experiences will sooner or later include your ex, and you don't need to be reminded of her right now.

The advantage of new friends is they have no shared experiences and therefore have no interest in talking about her. They can also turn you on to things you never knew about or considered doing.

Join a divorced men's support group.

One of the most advantageous things that happened to me is that I met other men who had already gone through a divorce or were in the process. At a divorced men's group you might run into someone who has already been through what you are going through and has a job that is similar to yours, makes around the same amount of money, was married as long as you were and has about the same number of kids.

The information this person could provide is invaluable! In this book I can only address generalities. I have no idea if you are the president of a major corporation or a guy making minimum wage. How a divorce plays out depends heavily on your station in life, so having input from someone who has been where you are in now, and can tell you what you should do and what to expect, could make the process a lot easier.

Go to and throw parties.

This might be a whole new ballgame for you. Maybe you weren't the party type and only attended when the wife dragged you along. Maybe you don't like parties because too often the people there were dull, shallow and boring. And yes, there are few things in life more draining then being roped into a conversation with someone prattling on about some subject you couldn't care less about.

But this is the new you and this is your new life. And for it to be successful you must become somebody people enjoy talking to, somebody people like being around.

To some this comes naturally. They're funny, engaging and interesting. This is your goal. If you already are that person, good for you, keep at it. If you aren't, then learn to be.

That's right, learn to be.

Over your lifetime you've learned a number of skills that were necessary to improve your life. Maybe some business courses, computer courses, basic mechanics, you get the point. Now it's time to learn new social skills and become more proficient at interpersonal relationships.

This is necessary for a number of reasons. First, the more people you meet, the more likely you're going to come in contact with someone who's fascinating and one you'd like to get to know better.

But you need to be fascinating too for them to want to spend time with you.

So develop your social skills. Read self improvement books, Books like, "How to Make Friends and Influence People" and "How You can be the Life of the Party. And attend self improvement seminars that focus on acquiring these skills.

The payoff is the opening of a whole new world. Since my divorce, I've been invited to go up in a glider with a group of experienced pilots, deep sea fishing in the Florida Keys, play in a rock band, film and edit videos, and ride with middle-aged motorcycle enthusiasts from New York to Tennessee.

Upgrade yourself.

Now that the divorce is final and you know exactly where your finances are, it's time to address all the personal things you've been putting off. And since you're starting a new life, you want to look your best.

First off, how are your teeth? If they are in need of repair, find a good dentist and have them taken care of. Once done, how does your hair look? If it's grey or white and is making you look old and tired instead of distinguished, start coloring it. If you're losing your hair, start shaving your head or contact one of the many hair replacement centers and get an appraisal and references. This is the 21st century and the day of the bad rug has been kicked to the curb. Besides, you paid your dues, and there is nothing wrong with you laying out some money to look and feel better.

Plastic surgery.

It's not just for women anymore, and it's not all that expensive either. (Although prices do vary with the procedure.) Maybe it's time to give the old heave-ho to the sagging double chin, the jowls and the bags under the eyes.

The wardrobe.

Must likely it was the ex who picked out your clothes, now it's your turn, but keep in mind, if you have no talent for fashion then you need to find somebody who does. This doesn't mean you'll be parading down the catwalk, what I mean is if you know someone who dresses well and has good taste, find out where they get their clothes and ask their opinion on what they think you should wear.

The sports car:

I suspected you knew we'd get to this eventually. It's the flagship of male menopause, of middle age crazy. Countless jokes have been made about it. Middle aged women roll their eyes, young men snigger.

Nuts to them. If you want one and can afford it, then go ahead and buy one! It doesn't have to be a Porsche or Ferrari. There are many fine looking sports cars in a reasonable price range. And most of all, you deserve one. After all those years you putting the needs of the wife and kids first (ever notice that's it's always the wife who gets to drive the newer car?) you can finally treat yourself to that fine looking vehicle you've always wanted.

I did and the first time I opened her up on the highway my heart literally sang! I had the eight speaker surround sound stereo cranking and the tack tapping the red line as I shifted. My hair was blowing, my eyes were wide and my smile ran from ear to ear.

A week after I bought it, I was stopped for a light when a kid about 12 walked in front of my car. His jaw dropped as he eyed my sweet ride and gasped, "Cool car!"

I never understood the allure when I was younger, but now I do. And every time I see a guy my age behind the wheel of a sharp looking car, I give him the thumbs up. You earned it, my friend, so enjoy every minute behind the wheel!

Chapter 11

Don't let anyone live in your head who isn't paying rent.

The meaning of that saying is simple. The rent people pay when you think of them is the smiles and good feeling you experience when they pop into your thoughts.

When your ex shows up in your thoughts, is she bringing any smiles to your face? No? Then it's eviction time. Train yourself not to think of her and when she does slip in, divert your attention to something else, because it's keeping you from accomplishing the one last mighty feat, and that is to become a member of that 'Shining City on the Hill'.

And the name of that city?

Indifference.

You will never succeed in creating your new life until you stop hating your ex. The reason for this is that the opposite of love isn't hate; it's indifference.

If a reasonable amount of time has passed for you to come to grips with the hurt she caused and you've rejoined the living by getting together with your new friends, are enjoying your new hobbies and have taken a dip or two in the dating pool, then the time has come to jettison any remaining feelings you have for her. Love, hate, jealousy, anger, empathy, worry, envy, any and all has got to go. It will be very difficult sure, but in order to truly begin your new life you must get to the point where news of her winning the lottery or getting remarried or even passing away has little to no effect, any more than say, hearing the same news about a girl you once went steady with in high school.

You take a moment to reflect, then continue on with whatever you were doing. It's just that simple. You no longer are the man who loved her, cherished her and took care of her. You are a new man and have begun a new life. Embrace it, and don't let any of the misery from the past have any place in it.

The Recap.

Okay, you've made it through this book and have learned how to deal with the situation when, after being married for over twenty-plus years, your wife suddenly becomes hateful, and vindictive toward you.

You respond to this by…

Convincing her to see a doctor to make sure this personality change has no medical basis.

Find out if she has any interest in continuing the marriage. (Ignore what she says, it's what she does that answers that question.)

Stop blaming yourself, her actions are not a response to anything you have done.

Keep your eye on that joint savings account.

Get the guns out of the house.

CONSULT A LAWYER!

Don't let her or her lawyer goad you into acting irrationally or out of anger.

Keep a tight leash on your drinking, watch out for depression.

Talk to your doctor about getting healthy and back in shape

Remember the 5 women to avoid at all costs.

Follow the steps to starting a new life. Yes it will take awhile but it's worth the effort.

Move on and don't look back.

Why I wrote this book

When this book comes out I have no doubt I will be accused of being an angry, vindictive, woman-hating misogynist whose own hateful personality was the cause for the breakup of my marriage, but I'm not and it wasn't. I was married for 25 wonderful years and then it ended.

When it did, I began hanging around and talking with other divorced men my age and was amazed at the commonality in all the breakups. In so many cases, the guy had no idea the wife wanted out and was still trying to figure out why, when the judge banged the gavel and granted the divorce.

I figured one of us should tell all the other middle-aged guys that they aren't alone and that after the smoke has cleared there is still a lot of life ahead.

So I decided to be that guy.

I got my life back on track because I accepted that my old life was gone, there was nothing I could do about it and that I had two choices. I could get busy livin' or I could get busy dyin'

Livin' is better.

So there you go, friend. Don't expect the process to go swiftly or smoothly. These things never do, there will be dark days and situations you will have to deal with that are not described in this book, but at least now you have a general idea what to expect and how to protect yourself.

If you have any comments or stories you'd like to share regarding your own personal experiences with middle age divorce you can e-mail me at czar@aripublishing.com In the meantime why not visit my publisher at www.aripublishing.com and have a look at my other books.

www.ingramcontent.com/pod-product-compliance
Lightning Source LLC
Chambersburg PA
CBHW071420040426
42445CB00012BA/1229